Let's Celebrate

NEW YEAR'S DAY

BY Barbara deRubertis

Kane Press
New York

For activities and resources for this book and others in the HOLIDAYS & HEROES series, visit: www.kanepress.com/holidays-and-heroes

Text copyright © 2018 by Barbara deRubertis
Photographs/images copyrights: Cover: © Tom Wang/Shutterstock; page 1: © Fotohunter/Shutterstock; page 3: © Dotshock/Shutterstock; page 4: © Designua/Shutterstock; page 5: © Line Tale/Shuttersock; page 6: © Wwing/iStock; page 7: © Anastasiya Matvienko/Shutterstock; pages 8–9 background: © Audrey Kuzmin/Shutterstock; page 8 top inset: © Chronicle/Alamy Stock Photo; page 8 bottom inset: © Interfoto/Alamy Stock Photo; page 10: © Nastasic/iStock; page 10 inset: © Gilmanshin/Shutterstock; page 10 sidebar: © Audrey Kuzmin/Shutterstock; page 11 left: © Dmitr1ch/Shutterstock; page 11 right: © Tamara Tas/Shutterstock; page 12: © Age Fotostock/Alamy Stock Photo; page 13: © Everett Historical/Shutterstock; page 14: © Library of Congress, Prints & Photographs Division, LC-USZC4-5584; page 15: © Viktorua Hodos/Shutterstock; page 16: © David Cohen 156/Shutterstock; page 17: © Monkey Business Images/Shutterstock; page 18: © Richard Levine/Alamy Stock Photo; page 19: © Liang Sen Xinhua News Agency/Newscom; page 19 background: Library of Congress, Prints and Photographs Division, LC-DIG-det-4a16709; page 20: © Courtesy of the author; page 21 top: © Germán Vogel/Alamy Stock Photo; page 21 bottom: © Chris Greenberg/UPI/Newscom; page 22: © Chonnanit/Shutterstock; © page 23 top: © Winston Tan/Shutterstock; page 23 inset: © rmnddrr/Shutterstock; page 24 left: © i7do/Shutterstock; page 24 right: © Kobby Dagan/Shutterstock; page 25: © gagarych/Shutterstock; page 26: © Richard Levine/Alamy Stock Photo; page 27: © anouchka/iStock; page 28 left: © Kit Leong/Shutterstock; page 28 right: © Rawpixel.com/Shutterstock; page 29: © Vesna Cvorovic/Shutterstock; page 30: © vm2002/Shutterstock; page 31: © Aaraujo/Shutterstock; page 32: © Martin Dimitrov/iStock, back cover: © Martin Dimitrov/iStock,
All due diligence has been conducted in identifying copyright holders and obtaining permissions.

Library of Congress Cataloging-in-Publication Data

Names: deRubertis, Barbara, author.
Title: Let's Celebrate New Year's Day / by Barbara deRubertis.
Description: New York : Kane Press, 2018. | Series: Holidays & heroes.
Identifiers: LCCN 2018007790 (print) | LCCN 2018015898 (ebook) | ISBN 9781635920598 (ebook) | ISBN 9781635920574 (reinforced library binding : alk. paper) | ISBN 9781635920581 (pbk. : alk. paper)
Subjects: LCSH: New Year--Juvenile literature.
Classification: LCC GT4905 (ebook) | LCC GT4905 .D47 2018 (print) | DDC 394.2614--dc23
LC record available at https://lccn.loc.gov/2018007790

10 9 8 7 6 5 4 3 2 1

First published in the United States of America in 2018 by Kane Press, Inc.
Printed in China

Book Design and Photograph/Image Research: Maura Taboubi

Visit us online at www.kanepress.com.

Like us on Facebook
facebook.com/kanepress

Follow us on Twitter
@KanePress

When people change their calendar from one year to the next, they like to celebrate! In fact, people have been celebrating the beginning of a new year for thousands of years.

But a new year does not have to begin in the middle of winter on the first day of a month called January.

That's because people living at different times, in different parts of the world, have had different calendars. And they still do!

HOW WE MEASURE TIME

When people first began to make calendars, they used some ideas based on science.

- A **day** is the time it takes Earth to make one complete rotation—about 24 hours.
- A **month** is based on the time it takes the Moon to travel around Earth. The word *month* comes from *moon*. Each moon cycle is about 29 and 1/2 days.
- A **year** is the time it takes Earth to travel around the sun. Each year is about 365 days.

The summer solstice is the longest day of the year. The winter solstice is the shortest. On the spring and autumn equinoxes, night and day are *equal* in length.

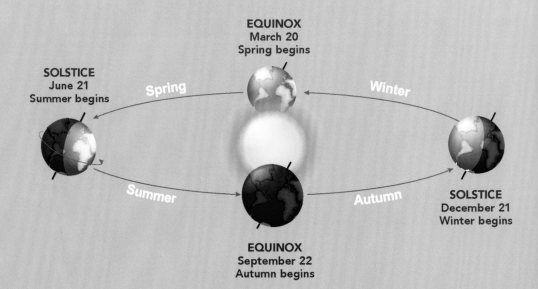

EARTH'S SEASONS

EQUINOX
March 20
Spring begins

Spring

Winter

SOLSTICE
June 21
Summer begins

Summer

Autumn

SOLSTICE
December 21
Winter begins

EQUINOX
September 22
Autumn begins

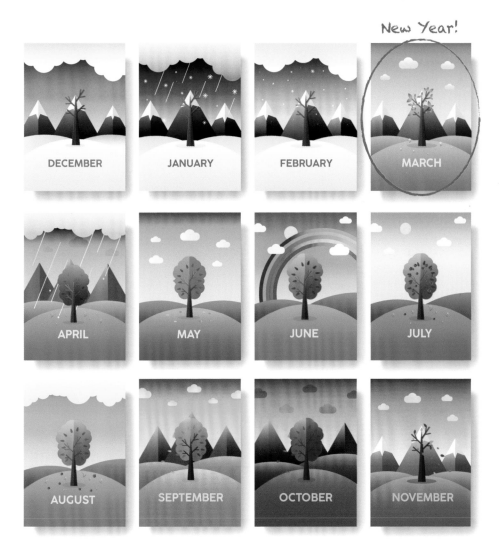

ANCIENT CALENDARS

Ancient peoples often began their new year on the first day of spring—around March 20.

But other people began their new year on the first day of fall, on the first day of winter, or at other times of the year.

Native American Calendars

Early Native American calendars were based on moon cycles, or months.

Different tribes had different names for the full moons. Each one was named after something important that happened in nature during that moon cycle.

So moons had names such as Snow Moon, Flower Moon, and Harvest Moon. Some tribes still use their own names for the months today.

Wolf Moon

Snow Moon

Worm Moon

Pink Moon

Flower Moon

Strawberry Moon

Thunder Moon

Sturgeon Moon

Harvest Moon

Hunter Moon

Beaver Moon

Cold Moon

Romulus's Calendar

Legends say the earliest Roman calendar was made by the first king of Rome, Romulus. It was created about 2,700 years ago. The new year began on March 1 and had ten months.

Some months were named after Roman gods and goddesses. And some months were just named after the numbers that matched their place in the calendar. How many of these names look familiar to you?

1. MARTIUS—MARS (GOD OF WAR)
2. APRILIS—APHRODITE (GODDESS OF LOVE)
3. MAIUS—MAIA (GODDESS OF SPRING)
4. JUNIUS—JUNO (QUEEN OF THE GODS)
5. QUINTILIS—QUINQUE (FIVE)
6. SEXTILIS—SEX (SIX)
7. SEPTEMBER—SEPTEM (SEVEN)
8. OCTOBER—OCTO (EIGHT)
9. NOVEMBER—NOVEM (NINE)
10. DECEMBER—DECEM (TEN)

Romulus

Numa

Numa's Calendar

According to legend, the second king of Rome was Numa. He added two new months to the calendar, *Januarius* and *Februarius.*

Now there were twelve months instead of ten. So the months numbered five through ten became months seven through twelve!

1. JANUARIUS—JANUS (GOD OF BEGINNINGS)
2. FEBRUARIUS—FEBRUA (AN IMPORTANT FESTIVAL)
3. MARTIUS—MARS (GOD OF WAR)
4. APRILIS—APHRODITE (GODDESS OF LOVE)
5. MAIUS—MAIA (GODDESS OF SPRING)
6. JUNIUS—JUNO (QUEEN OF THE GODS)
7. QUINTILIS—QUINQUE (FIVE)
8. SEXTILIS—SEX (SIX)
9. SEPTEMBER—SEPTEM (SEVEN)
10. OCTOBER—OCTO (EIGHT)
11. NOVEMBER—NOVEM (NINE)
12. DECEMBER—DECEM (TEN)

Julian Calendar

Seven hundred years later, Julius Caesar was the first ruler of the Roman Empire. He introduced *another* new calendar. We still use this calendar today, with only small changes.

In his honor, the name of the month Quintilius (his birth month) was changed to Julius.

Julius Caesar

The Roman Empire

Did you know the letter *j* wasn't invented until the 1500s? That means *Julius Ceasar* was originally spelled with the letter *i*, as in *Iulius Caesar*. Imagine having months like Ianuary, Iune, and Iuly!

The second ruler of the Roman Empire was Augustus Caesar. So the Romans changed the name of the month Sextilis to Augustus. How familiar are the names of the months now?

1. JANUARIUS
2. FEBRUARIUS
3. MARTIUS
4. APRILIS
5. MAIUS
6. JUNIUS
7. JULIUS
8. AUGUSTUS
9. SEPTEMBER
10. OCTOBER
11. NOVEMBER
12. DECEMBER

Augustus Caesar

Gregorian Calendar

In the year 567, the beginning of the new year was changed from January 1 to another date. Why? Because the new year's celebrations on January 1 were getting too rowdy!

The year now began on a religious holiday such as Christmas or Easter. Leaders hoped this would make people behave better.

In 1582, a pope of the Catholic Church named Gregory the 13th restored January 1 as the first day of the new year.

People getting rowdy at the Festival of Fools!

American colonists in the 1700s

The British Empire—and its American colonies—adopted the Gregorian calendar in 1752. Making the switch meant that the year 1752 was only 280 days long!

OTHER CALENDARS IN USE TODAY

There are other countries and cultures around the world that have different calendars based on their own history or religion.

When people move to the United States from these countries, they sometimes bring their calendars. They use them alongside the Gregorian calendar, which has become the international standard.

Immigrants coming to America

The Hebrew Calendar and New Year

The year 2020 on the Gregorian calendar would be 5780 on the Hebrew, or Jewish, calendar. The Jewish New Year is called Rosh Hashanah. It usually falls in September, but sometimes in October.

Jewish people everywhere celebrate Rosh Hashanah Eve and Rosh Hashanah. This holiday honors the birthday of the world.

Celebrating Rosh Hashanah

An Orthodox Jewish boy blows the shofar for Rosh Hashanah.

A ram's horn—called a *shofar*—is blown at the beginning of both days and during religious services held each morning. The shofar announces that a new year is beginning, and God has again been crowned king of the world.

Special foods are served at the family dinner on Rosh Hashanah. First, round loaves of challah bread are blessed and served with honey. Then slices of apple dipped in honey are served. The focus of the meal is on sweet foods because the blessing asks for "a good and sweet year."

Making challah bread

The Persian Calendar and New Year

The Persian calendar is almost 3,000 years old, and it has had many changes.

Its new year begins on the first day of spring—on or near March 20. The year 1399 on the Persian calendar begins in March 2020 on the Gregorian calendar.

The first day of the Persian new year is called *Norooz*, which means "New Day." It is a public holiday in many places that were once part of the Persian Empire. TV and radio stations broadcast a countdown to the exact second when the new year begins.

Celebrating Norooz at the Persian Parade in New York City

The country once called Persia is now called Iran. Iranian Americans living in the U.S. celebrate the holiday in many traditional ways.

On the Wednesday before Norooz, people build bonfires and jump over them. This ancient tradition represents replacing the old year's problems with new warmth and energy.

Leaping over a fire for Norooz

Many families set up a traditional *Haft Seen* (or "Seven S") table. The Persian word for each of the seven items on the table begins with the letter *S*. Each item symbolizes something wished for in the new year.

The table might also display decorated eggs, a live goldfish, gold coins, a mirror, candles, poetry books, and flowers. The Haft Seen table is where the family gathers for the official arrival of the new year.

During the thirteen days of Norooz, families and friends plan short visits to each other's homes. On the last day of the holiday, people usually celebrate with an outdoor picnic.

A family in Washington State celebrates the 13th day of Norooz.

Above: A Haft Seen table in the White House. Can you find the "Seven S" items on the table? 1. Sabzeh (green sprouts) 2. Serkeh (vinegar) 3. Senjed (dried Persian olive) 4. Seer (garlic) 5. Seeb (apple) 6. Somaq (dark red spice) 7. Samanu (wheat pudding). The table may also include Sekkeh (coins), Sonbol (hyacinth flowers), and live goldfish.

The Chinese Calendar and New Year

Chinese New Year is a major holiday in China and in other countries in Asia. It is also celebrated by Chinese Americans in the U.S.

Chinese New Year's Day always falls between January 21 and February 20 on the Gregorian calendar. The Gregorian year 2020 is the year 4718 on the Chinese calendar.

The years are named for animals in a set, twelve-year cycle. Some people believe these animals influence the personalities of people born in their years.

Rat (creative, friendly)
2008, 2020, 2032

Ox (loyal, determined)
2009, 2021, 2033

Tiger (sensitive, brave)
2010, 2022, 2034

Rabbit (pleasing, peace-loving)
2011, 2023, 2035

Dragon (charming, full of fun)
2012, 2024, 2036

Snake (wise, loving)
2013, 2025, 2037

Horse (intelligent, fearless)
2014, 2026, 2038

Sheep (gentle, compassionate)
2015, 2027, 2039

Monkey (smart, adventurous)
2016, 2028, 2040

Rooster (generous, trustworthy)
2017, 2029, 2041

Dog (protective, faithful)
2018, 2030, 2042

Pig (kind, generous)
2019, 2031, 2043

Above: Fireworks in New York for Chinese New Year
Right: A red lantern

Preparations for the Chinese New Year begin seven days before New Year's Eve. Decorations are usually red—the color of luck and happiness.

- Red envelopes are filled with gifts of money.
- Good wishes written on "lucky red" paper are pasted on doors.
- Red paper cutouts are attached to windows.
- Paper lanterns are hung inside and outside.

On New Year's Eve, a feast is prepared for a family reunion. As soon as the clock strikes midnight, colorful displays of fireworks begin.

CELEBRATING THE NEW YEAR IN THE U.S.

New Year's Eve

New Year's Eve, on December 31, is widely celebrated in the U.S. Parties, concerts, and special events are held during the evening to "ring out the old year and ring in the new."

Millions of people turn on live broadcasts to watch the huge crowds gathered for the "ball drop" above Times Square in New York City. At one minute before midnight, the countdown begins. A giant crystal ball is slowly lowered down a 77-foot pole. It reaches the bottom at exactly midnight.

Thousands of people celebrate New Year's Eve in Times Square. After New York, midnight arrives in Chicago, Denver, Los Angeles, Anchorage, and finally in Honolulu.

The ball drop is immediately followed by fireworks. Musicians play "Auld Lang Syne." At midnight, it is a tradition for people to hug and kiss their loved ones.

The celebration of the new year then "rolls" westward through five more time zones.

New Year's Day

New Year's Day is a federal holiday. Special television programs are shown, including the Tournament of Roses Parade and football games.

Above: A float at the Rose Parade
Right: A family watching a game

Some people make New Year's Resolutions. They think of something about themselves they want to improve or something they want to achieve. Then they make a "resolution" . . . and a plan to meet their goal. They try to stick to the plan every day!

There are traditional "lucky" foods that many people eat on New Year's Day in the U.S. The foods are supposed to bring good health, success, and happiness in the year ahead.

Some of these food traditions began in the South. The most famous one is black-eyed peas!

Black-eyed peas in a southern dish called Hoppin' John

Many Mexican Americans eat grapes as they ring in the New Year.

Many Mexican Americans carry on the tradition of eating 12 grapes, one at a time, as the clock is striking midnight on New Year's Eve. This is said to bring good luck for all 12 months of the new year *if* you finish before the final chime sounds.

Italian Americans sometimes eat lentils on New Year's Day. In Italy, the small, round lentils looked like Roman coins. So eating lentils was thought to bring wealth and success.

German Americans eat pickled herring. Asian Americans eat soba noodles. Turkish Americans eat pomegranates. The list goes on!

New Year's is a holiday that can be shared by everyone, everywhere. There are so many interesting traditions! And so many ways to celebrate!

Every time we say "Happy New Year," we are part of the long line of people in history who wished for a good year ahead for themselves, their friends, and their family.